INTERIORS ARCHITECTURE

THE MOST INNOVATIVE PROJECTS OF THE YEAR

INTERIORS ARCHITECTURE

THE MOST INNOVATIVE PROJECTS OF THE YEAR

LOFT

Editorial coordination: Cristina Paredes Benítez

Texts: Loft Publications

Art director: Mireia Casanovas Soley

Design: Nil Solà Serra

Editorial project:

2007 © **LOFT Publications**
Via Laietana 32, 4° Of. 92
08003 Barcelona, Spain
Tel.: +34 932 688 088
Fax: +34 932 687 073
loft@loftpublications.com
www.loftpublications.com

ISBN: 978-84-95832-86-3

Printed in China

INTRODUCTION

INTRODUCTION
INTRODUCTION

These days the panorama of the design of home interiors is dominated by the highly interesting results created by author architecture. Based on this creative concept, the new technologies have monopolized a determining role thanks to which the wildest desires of owners and the wildest caprices of some architects can be fulfilled.

Residential architecture is a paradigmatic typology belonging to a concrete moment, unlimited in its evolution, always open to investigation. The field of experimentation can hardly be said to be narrow and embraces both the use of materials and the use of the space itself. It is a mode that also investigates new forms of concordance between the changes produced in family nuclei and in the current modus vivendi, as well as the new functions of each one of these spaces. Light, in spite of not being a tangible element, is certainly a fundamental resource in these spaces and, not infrequently, is the base from which a home is planned, either by way of its abundance or its absence.

Today, private residences possess an infinite range of designs, not only exteriors but interiors as well, thanks to the wide variety of materials and to the ecological revolution giving rise to the possibility of incorporating new architectural elements and solutions.

Then again, both the design of furniture and the chromatism used are important in reflecting the personality of the owners and thus making clear their tastes and preferences.

Interiors Architecture includes a selection of contemporary international homes combining both traditional spaces (with new architectural solutions) and the new and revolutionary concepts of the home. The constructions displayed in this book exist in both urban and rural spaces, thus opening up another research route: the integration of the house into the surrounding environment.

INTERIORS ARCHITECTURE

ROSENBERG RESIDENCE

Architects: Belmont Freeman Architects

Photographer: © Christopher Wesnofske

Location: New York, United States   Surface: 3,000 sq. ft.

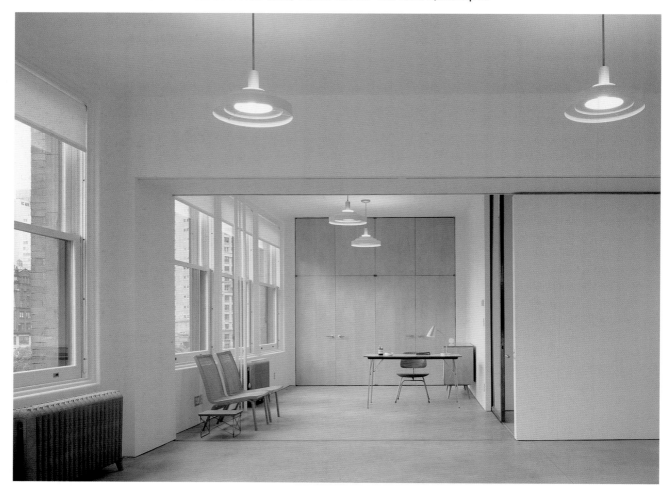

Located in Lower Manhattan, this dwelling is one more example of an old space from the twentieth century dedicated to commercial activities that has been refurbished to become a comfortable residence. The extreme height of the ceilings along with the existence of different levels makes it possible to experiment with the space.

The Rosenberg residence, in an early twentieth-century commercial building in Lower Manhattan that was converted to residential use during the 1980s, makes the most of its dual heritage. Placing the dwelling and studio on different levels has enabled the users to enjoy specific, distinct environments within the same apartment.

The project involves two newly restored levels containing an office, studio, and home for an art lover. The relationship between the two units played a prominent role and led the architects to develop a plan that paradoxically joins and divides the two levels through the use of specific materials.

On the upper floor the dwelling contains a living room, kitchen, and two bedrooms. The exterior wall, which is free of partitions, admits generous light from the north. The lower level, which holds the office and studio, features a restored, sandblasted concrete floor covered in zinc casting. Two mobile screens, one made of plasterboard and the other of translucent glass, make it easy to rearrange the apartment. The two levels are linked by a staircase typical of naval constructions that separates the day and night areas.

1. Living room
2. Kitchen
3. Bedroom
4. Bathroom
5. Office
6. Study

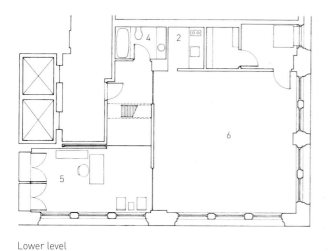

Lower level

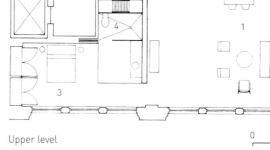

Upper level

0 1 2

The upper level houses the living room, the kitchen and both bedrooms. The access to this floor is made by metallic staircase, typical of naval constructions.

CIATTI HOUSE

CIATTI
HOUSE

Architect: Claudio Nardi

Photographers: © Estudio Santi Caleca

Location: Florence, Italy   Surface: 8,870 sq. ft.

The extensive use of skylights brings abundant light into this villa near the city of Florence.

☐ The building that houses this home is situated in the area of Lastra a Signa, near the city of Florence. It is immersed in the classical landscape of Tuscany and its gently rolling hills, its olive trees, and the towers and villages in the distance. Already before the renovation, the construction had an air of solemnity and the distinction of a noble palace, thanks to the simplicity of style and materials, which are typical to the region. Nevertheless, it lacks the usual complex compositional realization, which results in the austerity and purity of its linear forms.

The project, specifically its interior, is based on the creation of a double-height central nucleus, which is submerged in natural light that descends from a series of skylights. These symmetric apertures act as a reference for the austere characteristic of the building, inside of which the rooms and functions are distributed over two levels. The ground floor contains the living room, kitchen and reading area, while the first floor contains the bedrooms, bathroom and lounge. The austere white spaces are interspersed with traditional Italian architecture, such as the vaulted brick ceiling in the bathroom.

The architect chose natural materials such as linestone and wedge wood compositional elements, including the stairs, door frames, floors and walls. At the same time he attempted to blend the fireplaces, light fixtures and paneling into a neutral background free of any over-charged design elements.

The living room occupies a space below the ceiling. Upstairs, the catwalks enable visual connection between the bedrooms and the ground floor.

1. Entrance
2. Living room
3. Kitchen
4. Dining room
5. Office
6. Bathroom
7. Laundry room

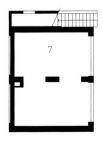 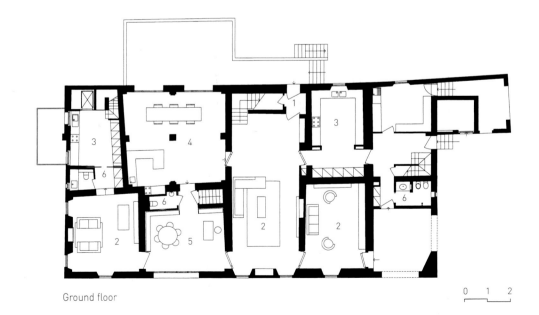

Ground floor

0 1 2

Conceptually, the architect wished to re-interpret the material minimalism of volume and form in a contemporary language; accentuating void, light and shadow.

1. Bedroom
2. Bathroom
3. Living room
4. Office
5. Guest house

First floor

0   1   2

The coexistence of contemporary and traditional becomes evident in this bathroom, where a stainless steel counter lies underneath an old roof structure.

Longitudinal section

Transversal section

LIPSCHUTZ-JONES
APARTMENT

LIPSCHUTZ-JONES APARTMENT

Architects: Frank Lupo, Daniel Rowen

Photographer: © Michael Moran

Location: New York, United States   Surface: 1,600 sq. ft.

This space serves to contain the home of a couple who work as stock market agents and a work space where computers and other electronic communication systems can be used.

☐ The Lipschutz-Jones apartment, in Lower Manhattan, was designed for a pair of Wall Street stockbrokers.

A two-story living room is situated at the front while two levels at the back, next to the wall that defines the building's internal corridor, accommodate the essential activities. A high, narrow passage connects the rooms and partitions off different areas. The bedroom lies above the kitchen, and the office sits on the other side, below the master bath. This means that the work area is separated from the bedroom but can be seen from the kitchen and central corridor. Along with the office computers, six screens are interspersed throughout the apartment.

A steel staircase leads to the second floor, where a beam reduces the impact of the bare space created by the corridor, and doubles as a bookcase. In the rest of the home, a wide palette of materials—including maple wood, marble, granite, and translucent glass—gives the project strong visual character.

The clients essentially desired an integrated room to house sophisticated computer and communication systems from which to monitor the international market at any time.

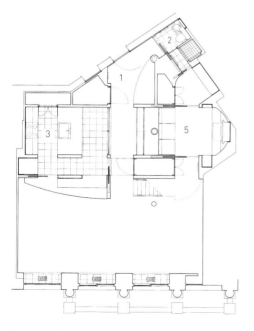
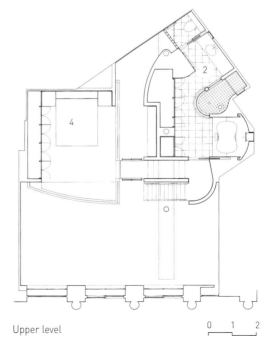

1. Entrance
2. Bathroom
3. Kitchen
4. Bedroom
5. Living room

Lower level

Upper level

0 1 2

LOFT IN PIMLICO

LOFT IN PIMLICO

Architects: Farshid Moussavi, Alejandro Zaera

Photographer: © Valerie Bennett

Location: London, United Kingdom   Surface: 1,930 sq. ft.

Given this desirable setting, the architects exploited the features of the loft to the hilt. Some 645 square feet of floor space was gained by creating a mezzanine level that holds a bedroom that can be divided by means of sliding panels, a bathroom, and bookshelves visible from the main space.

Although architects Farshid Moussavi and Alejandro Zaera work at home only part-time, their multifunctional space has been included here because it merges public and private activities and rooms for night or daytime use. The L-shaped loft in the London neighborhood of Pimlico has ceilings that are nearly 16 feet high, with a somewhat shorter wing leading directly to the street.

The palette of materials was restricted to give the project a feeling of unity and to avoid detracting from the inherent quality of the space. All the walls and ceilings were painted white, except the end wall of the kitchen, which was finished in slate. Wide, solid oak tiles were perfect for the floor.

The solid metal columns of the large central space are reminiscent of the industrial origins of lofts. In this project, the beams subtly divide the dining area from the lounge.

1. Studio
2. Bathroom
3. Bedroom
4. Dining room
5. Kitchen
6. Living room

Mezzanine

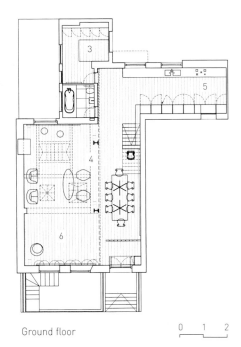

Ground floor

0 1 2

A great deal of surface area was gained by creating a mezzanine level that holds a bedroom that can be divided by means of sliding panels, a bathroom, and bookshelves visible from the main space.

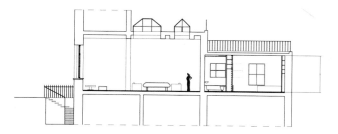

Transversal section

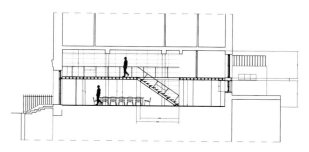

Longitudinal section

ANTIQUARIAN'S LOFT

Interior designer: The owner
Photographer: © Andrea Martiradonna

Location: Venice, Italy   Surface: 1,935 sq. ft.

A combination of Asian style and Italian tradition characterizes this loft designed by an antique collector.

☐ Located amidst a dense urban fabric of warehouses that was once the site of small industries and close to a large Venetian church, this loft was once a leading nineteenth century casting-metal factory. Its industrial features were preserved and combined with carefully chosen materials to create an ultimately open-plan living space.

Supervised by the owner himself, the restoration project intended to maintain the existing structure when transforming the space into a home that would respond to the necessities of its tenants. After restoring the original structure, the considerable ceiling height led to the construction of a mezzanine that would contain the more intimate places like the bedrooms. The mezzanine is also a catwalk from which to contemplate the views of the church dome and the patio paved in stone. An antique wood monetiere with intricate carving coated with gold-leaf sits next to a pair of old suitcases, adding a touch of classicism and vintage to the space. The wood and metal staircase leads down to a small studio area partitioned off from the surrounding living and dining area. All installations are concealed beneath the birchwood floors.

The furnishings are designed by the owner, save for the sixteenth century Iberian monetiere. The bedrooms and interior garden have a distinct Japanese flavor that can be detected in the dining area as well. Solid wooden trusses, brick walls and glass doors guarantee a diaphanous space full of authenticity and character. A subtle mixture of styles generates an ultimately Italian feel within this post-industrial loft in Venice.

The dining area and adjacent courtyard are examples of the Asian influence on the design.

The typically Italian kitchen looks onto the exterior through a series of windows.

From inside the loft, one can enjoy the view of a beautiful basilica, located just a few minutes away.

Loft in Plaza Mayor

Architect: Manuel Ocaña del Valle
Collaborators: Celia López Aguado, Laura Rojo
Photographer: © Alfonso Postigo

Location: Madrid, Spain   Surface: 1,075 sq. ft.

The relationships between the different spaces, the bedroom and the study, or the television room and the living room, are achieved with transparent elements, such as glass, or a simple curtain that can divide each zone. The decorative palette, in light tones, also unifies the space and emphasizes the feeling of spaciousness.

This project involved an irregularly formed apartment in an old building located in the center of Madrid. The structure was disorganized and had suffered significant damage and numerous "patch" renovations. The load-bearing walls were wide and presented variable strokes. The passageways were badly defined, and there were angles and projections that made it difficult to move around in a space with such great depth.

The architect restructured the space by creating a regular and orthogonal order. He reorganized the circulations in a space fragmented by sustaining walls that have an important structural function and also organize the space. The new distribution divided the loft into two large zones: a large, open one for the primary living space, and another one, with similar dimensions, that was broken down into smaller areas. A criterion for the renovation of these spaces was to respect the structural elements, since the overall state of the building was poor. The circulation was reorganized so the resident can appreciate the space as a whole. The materials and textures used for the remodeling reflect the concepts of the apartment's new structure. Woodwork was eliminated in order to free the apartment from the weight of its surroundings. Woodwork and metallic veneers for the furnishings and the doors were used to waterproof the humid zones. This project strengthened the role of the load-bearing walls. Not only structurally functional, they also organize the space. An irregular series of opaque and thick dividing panels gives the loft a new spatial distribution.

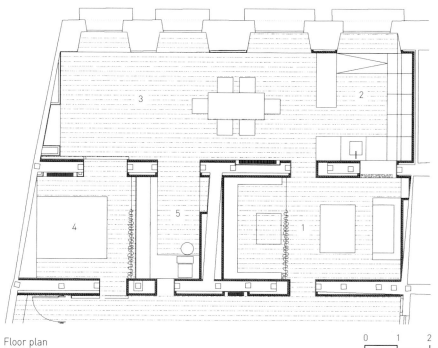

1. TV room
2. Kitchen
3. Dining room
4. Bedroom
5. Studio

Floor plan

0   1   2

Even though some elements of the original space were preserved, such as the dark wood platform, new materials transformed the character of the space by giving it a contemporary image. Designer furniture, like the chaise lounge by Le Corbusier upholstered in cowhide, complements the atmosphere. The stainless steel table, which serves as a counter in the kitchen and as an informal dining room table, is a folding sheet attached to the wall that makes for continuity.

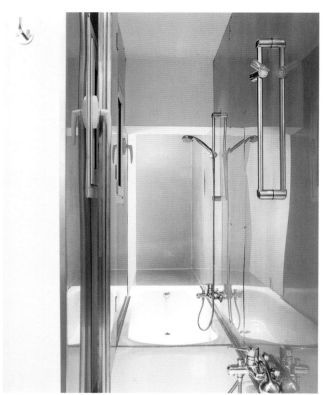

The openings in the walls create relationships between the various areas of the residence, such as the television room and the kitchen. The openings also take advantage of natural light to illuminate the spaces in the rear of the apartment.

PARK WEST APARTMENT

Architects: Bonetti Kozerski Studio
Collaborators: Arnold Chan/Isometrix (lighting);
I. Grace Company (contractor)

Photographer: © Matteo Piazza

Location: New York, United States   Surface: 7,795 sq. ft.

The apartment was refurbished with thoughts of the spectacular views the house offers of Central Park, in Manhattan. The objective was to connect the interior and the exterior to integrate the wide terraces into the totality of the space.

This huge apartment has several terraces to the north and south overlooking Central Park. The project features a master bedroom suite that includes a dressing room and bathroom gallery; a large living room and dining room, which are connected to the terraces with a stone platform that runs throughout; a meditation room and "spa" bathroom; a chef's kitchen and preparation kitchen/pantry; a house manager's office; and a maid's suite.

The apartment is furnished with custom furniture designed by Bonetti Kozerski Studio, Asian antique pieces, and some contemporary pieces. Floors in the public spaces feature cross-cut travertine in four-foot-square tiles, while the bathrooms use larger pieces of travertine on the walls and floors. Flooring in the master suite is a tatami-style wool sisal in a color matching the stone. The walls are highly polished Venetian stucco in an ivory color. The ceilings are custom-colored ivory paint.

The woodwork throughout the apartment is teak, with a dark-stained finish in the dining room and master bedroom. The kitchen features a combination of natural teak, stainless steel lower cabinets, frosted glass upper cabinets, and a basalt volcanic stone countertop.

Some of the architectural solutions were derived from the techniques employed in the full-size model that was built to verify the ambience of spaces, such as the lighting that originates from the floor to make the low ceilings look less oppressive (votive candles were used on the floor in the mock-up) or the back-lit linen walls. The lighting was designed by Arnold Chan from London's Isometrix, who had already collaborated with the architects on other projects.

Light streaming in from the windows and the interior fixtures radiates throughout the apartment, harmonically unifying the space.

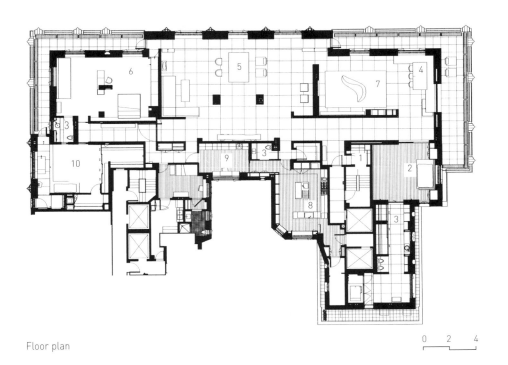

1. Entrance
2. Yoga's room
3. Bathroom
4. Dining room
5. Sitting room
6. Bedroom
7. TV room
8. Kitchen
9. Butler's area
10. Dressing room

Floor plan

0   2   4

ATTIC FOR A PUBLICIST

Architect: Arthur de Mattos Casas

Photographer: © Tuca Reinés

Location: São Paulo, Brazil   Surface: 3,440 sq. ft.

The client's private quarters have a landscaped terrace with views of the city. Due to the weight that the structure supporting the swimming pool and the plants had to bear, it had to be considerably reinforced. The studio on this level contains a fireplace, an office, and a bookcase.

    The apartment occupies the two top floors of a São Paulo building, and was designed for a famous publicist. Due to the fact that the number of occupants fluctuates, the dwelling was divided into three different zones. In the first place, the area serves the children who sporadically occupy these rooms. This includes the bedrooms and a room for the television and computer. This same floor accommodates the living area, salon, dining room, kitchen, and wash place. The floor above houses the client's private quarters, joined to a terrace with a swimming pool. The project involved no conceptual effort as far as domestic programs are concerned. Efforts here were directed toward placing different works of art and collector's pieces. The main objective was that all of these elements should be placed flexibly, without cluttering space—altering it while also embellishing it. Hence the fact that the pictures are hung from rails by steel cables that may be easily displaced. Furthermore, the objects were put into display cabinets so they would not obstruct the overall visual effect and would be highlighted as they deserve, thanks to specific protection and lighting in each case.

Arthur de Mattos Casas's architectural studio not only conceived of the space, but also produced some of the furniture elements for the project, in this case the rug and the dining room table. The apartment also contains design pieces: the dining room chairs are by Charles Eames, the lamp by Pierre Chareau, and the sofa by Jean-Michel Frank.

The staircase linking both floors consists of a white-painted metal structure to which wooden steps were attached. Although the materials and finishes coincide with those of the dwelling, this element appears sculptural and confers character on the space.

SAMPAOLI RESIDENCE
RESIDENCE

SAMPAOLI RESIDENCE

Architect: Claudio Caramel

Photographer: © Paolo Utimpergher

Location: Padua, Italy   Surface: 1,290 sq. ft.

The exact measurements of the design details of the interior architecture and the use of a certain type of furniture inside the space give this project a somewhat informal and casual appearance, though with truly contemporary taste.

Created inside an old print shop, formerly used as a carpentry warehouse, this loft is located in a building in the center of Padua, in northern Italy. Though the space conserved its original character, the architect created an atmosphere that more closely matches the typology of a traditional residence. The private spaces are defined by independent bedrooms, but the area that dominates the interior is a large room that groups the functions of the living room, dining room, and kitchen.

The atmosphere of this space is a well-balanced mix of technology and creativity. The result is subtle elegance. The clarity of the forms was achieved through an ingenious strategy to hide certain elements and highlight others. The main entrance is through a garage that leads to the studio or to the residence, resolving the issue of parking while creating an unusual and informal entrance. The space containing the living room, dining room, and kitchen is a large atmosphere bathed in light thanks to large windows and light-colored walls. As in the rest of the residence, traces of its former industrial use are visible, like the brick walls, the exposed tubes, the pillars painted white, and the band of glass blocks in the upper part. The sleeping zone is delimited by walls and doors, like in a conventional residence, and includes two bedrooms and two bathrooms. Other highlights are the small-format tiles and the faucets and bathroom fixtures designed by Philippe Starck.

This interior's casual and informal image was achieved through the combination of austere furnishings, pieces designed by the owner of the residence, and some industrial elements, like the metallic shelves for books and the kitchen cabinets.

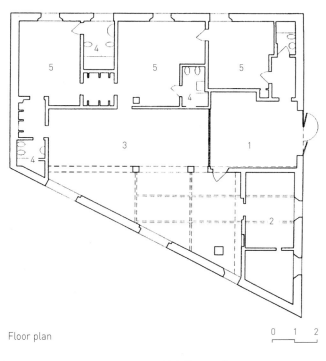

1. Access and garage
2. Kitchen
3. Dining room
4. Bathroom
5. Bedroom

Floor plan

0   1   2

Even though the private zones—the bedrooms and the bathrooms—are not part of the general space, they have a similar character. The humid zone of the bathroom is defined by mosaic that covers part of the walls, as if in a superimposed drawing.

O'NEILL APARTMENT

O'NEILL
APARTMENT
APARTMENT

Architects: EFM Design
Collaborators: Ira Frazin (project supervisor);
Andrew Ferguson, Chartwell Builders (contractors)
Photographer: © Michael O'Neill

Location: New York, United States   Surface: 1,989 sq. ft.

The design of the residence is divided between two wings of the L-shaped floor plan. In the long wing is a large well-lit space with big windows where the common rooms are located, while the bedrooms, their respective bathrooms, and a studio are in the short wing. At the intersection, a small hall directs the circulation of the occupants.

☐ The studio, led by Emanuela Frattini Magnusson, was commissioned to do this renovation in Lower Manhattan, which included reorganizing the living spaces as well as completly designing the installations, the finishes, and even some of the furniture pieces.

The dining room, the living room, and the kitchen share a solid wood parquet floor and white plaster walls. The finish on the kitchen cabinets matches the appliances and the stainless steel chairs. The austerity of the building materials harmonizes with some of the owner's furniture and objects, like the magnificent rustic dining room table, which is extremely sober, almost sculptural. The taste for mixing rustic with the exquisite can also be seen in the structure, where the concrete is exposed in some places, and covered with impeccable plaster in others.

The bedrooms and the bathrooms also aspire to the serenity of the other rooms of the house. Warm, bright materials were used in a light color range.

1. Entrance
2. Kitchen
3. Bedroom
4. Bathroom
5. Dining room
6. Studio
7. Living room
8. Dressing room

Floor plan

0 2 4

The common domestic areas, living room, dining room, and kitchen occupy a single well-lit space with large exterior windows.

The choice of materials was governed by strict coherence: the tones, colors, and brightness of all the architectural elements form a homogenous setting.

WINDMILL STREET

WINDMILL STREET

Architect: Guillaume Dreyfuss

Photographer: © David Pisani

Location: Valletta, Malta   Surface: 1,613 sq. ft.

Once the site of a windmill field, this nineteenth-century building was adapted to house a loft distributed over several levels.

The public zones are paved in a monolithic self-leveling concrete and resin floor and are characterized by the steel and expanded metal stairs and landings that divide the floor horizontally into two areas.

The vertical shaft creates a visual link between all floors, accentuating the verticality of the house, and provides the upper levels with a heightened sensation of open space.

The more private bedroom area is laid with solid and resilient materials like gray terrazzo. A floor-to-ceiling closet and mosaic tile surface delineates the master bathroom.

The large windows on the two façades afford sea views. They also provide natural light offering the residence a more complete lighting, enhanced by the predominantly white walls.

Its privileged emplacement and the oversize windows on both the lower and the upper level provide the loft with some incredible views.

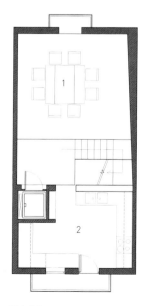

Third floor

Fourth floor

0 1 2

1. Dining room
2. Kitchen
3. Bedroom
4. Bathroom

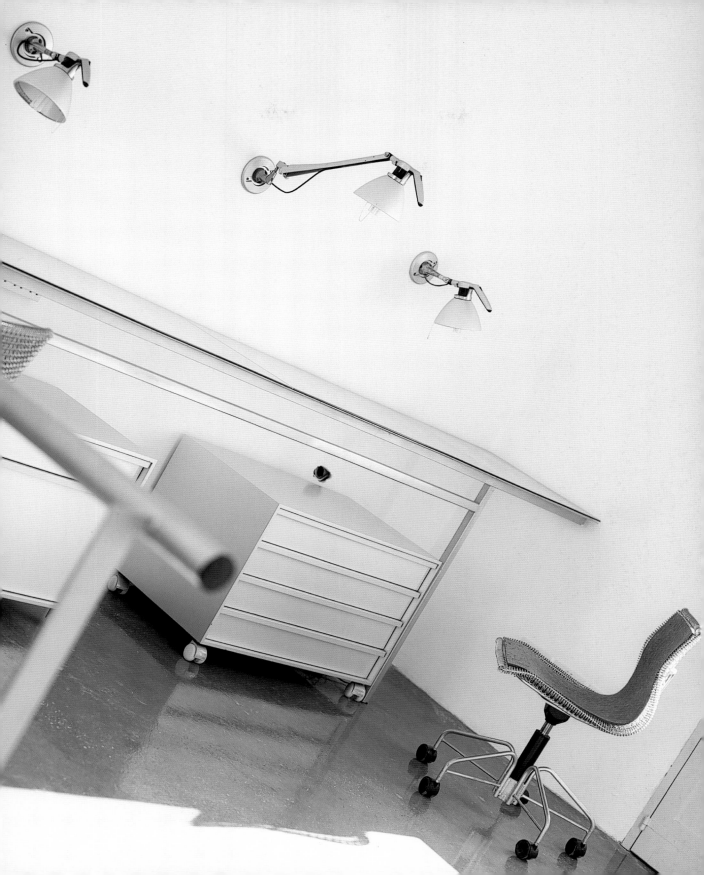

WEINSTEIN
LOFT

WEINSTEIN LOFT

Architects: Messana O'Rorke Architects
Collaborators: James Lee Construction (constructor)
Photographer: © Elizabeth Felicella

Location: New York, United States   Surface: 5,590 sq. ft.

Located in south Manhattan, this refurbished loft perfectly separates the common areas from the private ones, thus enabling the creation of diaphanous spaces without saturating the surface area, where different functions are combined.

Mixed function projects, in which both domestic and professional work is carried on, are recent phenomena that are rapidly becoming more common due to technological innovations and substantial improvements in communication. This was the case in the commission received by the Messana O'Rorke studio, which consisted of renovating an old industrial loft to convert it into a living space and an office with a clear corporate image. Furthermore, the client wanted to be able to exhibit his collection of mid-twentieth-century objects.

From the beginning, the architects decided to evoke the industrial legacy of the building. As such, the installations in the ceiling were left exposed, and the concrete floor was coated with only a plastic varnish which preserved the cracks as traces or scars left by the past manufacturing activities.

The ambiguous division between the living space and the office is made obvious by the translucent sliding doors that separate the two spaces, while the light that floods both areas dissolves the partitions. The double meaning was also used in the way the client's collection was exhibited, on one hand as practical objects, on the other as works of art.

Floor plan

0 2 4

1. Entrance
2. Graphic studio
3. Private work area
4. Copy room
5. Print workshop
6. Living room
7. Parlour
8. Kitchen
9. Bedroom
10. Bathroom

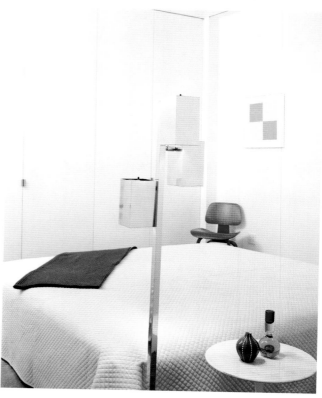

Despite the functional duality, the living space maintains an intimate character that is seen in the bedroom and bath, which, despite having an open plan, provide the necessary privacy to the users.

The character of the office is defined by wood furniture, designed by the architects, which was visually connected by covering the different pieces with melamine painted white, a solution that brought coherence and a professional image to the grouping. Occasionally, the work area is transformed into a perfect space for parties.

ARTIST'S LOFT

Architects: Massimo Imparato, Mauro Manfrin

Photographer: © Andrea Martiradonna

Location: Milan, Italy Surface: 1,500 sq. ft.

A mix of industrial, artistic and vintage elements characterizes this loft and studio. Above, two identical seventies armchairs sit below a ceiling of wooden beams.

One of a series of three renovations undertaken by the architects, this loft previously formed part of a 1920's industrial warehouse and was transformed into a home for an artist, a textile designer and their daughter. The elongated shape of the space and its high ceilings impelled the architects to divide it longitudinally and to create a mezzanine designated as an art studio. The architectural solutions are complemented by a decoration visibly influenced by the lifestyle of two artists.

The loft is 7.5 meters lengthwise and 16.5 meters in depth. Architects decided to place two divisions on either side. Upon entering, a white panel and sliding door conceal a narrow office and textile workshop from the entrance and living area. The half-height panel ensures a visual continuity within the space so that there is no rigid separation between the two areas. A bit further down, brick pillars mark the transition from public to private. A metal grated staircase leads to the art studio, which was furnished out of prefabricated white cement slabs laid over a metal structure. Beyond the stairs and a translucent screen, the kitchen and dining area share a common space, after which the daughter's bedroom is located. A full-height window incorporates a sliding door that opens up onto the courtyard, filling the lively and playful room with natural light during the day. The master bedroom is situated just next-door.

The framework of wooden beams on the roof structure is the most notable architectural feature of the loft. The roof structure dates back to the 1950's, in which a skylight was incorporated to bring light into the center of the space. Wood floors are varnished in white and decorative details were provided by the hand of the artists and the daily objects that surround their profession.

A half-height panel that incorporates a sliding door conceals the textile workshop without disconnecting it from the rest of the space. It also allows natural light to reach the work area. The entrance hall feels large and spacious mostly due to the high ceilings, the abundant daylight it receives and the light colors employed on the surfaces.

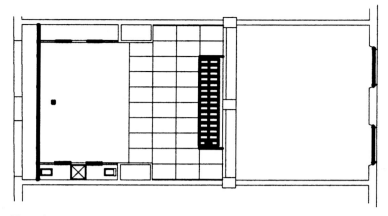

Mezzanine

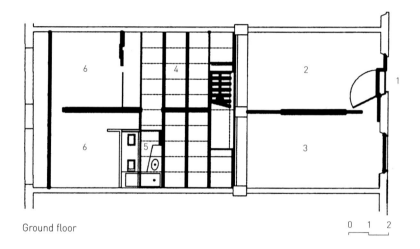

Ground floor

1. Entrance
2. Living room
3. Textile studio
4. Kitchen
5. Bathroom
6. Bedroom

0 1 2

Section

Many of the decorative objects, such as this Moroccan style lamp, were accumulated over the years throughout the owners' travels. Above, the white marble bath is prominent in the small bathroom. Right, the child's bedroom is playfully unkempt; bright colors are enhanced by the generous amount of light that enters through the floor-to-ceiling window.

A CONTINUAL PATH

A CONTINUAL PATH

Architect: Luis Cuartas
Collaborator: Guillermo Arias
Photographer: © Eduardo Consuegra

Location: Bogotá, Colombia   Surface: 968 sq. ft.

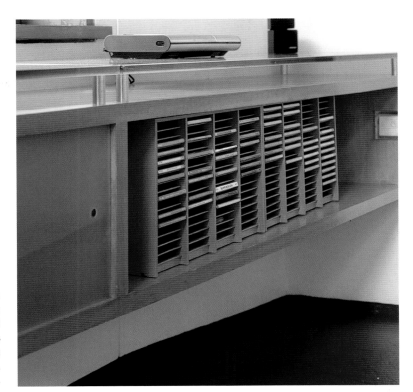

This project forms part of an integral reformation that two architects carried out on an old building in the center of Bogotá. The architects transformed the space into their personal residences. This particular project occupies the part of the building that previously contained the kitchen, the services, and the dining room.

☐ This project is part of the transformation of an old flat in two smaller dwellings. These share certain conditions, including the original structure and the tree-lined setting. These circumstances inspired similar operations in terms of alterations to the roof, an opening towards the tree-lined street, and the clearing of the interior space. On the other hand, each architect's distinct needs and architectural concepts brought about very different living spaces. After demolishing the existing walls, the architects envisioned the location of the new pieces that make up the residence. The goal was to create a continual space with diverse relationships between the different areas, and a circular, continual path that covers the entire residence. After crossing the entryway, the circulation offers two alternatives. On the left side, a table extends all the way to the door and invites entry into the kitchen. On the right side, a corridor containing a large bench and a bath integrated with the chimney, leads to the living room, which features unexpectedly high ceilings. From here, a steel stair leads to a walkway where there is a studio linked to a terrace. The chimney is open on both sides and paves the way to a more intimate zone with shorter ceilings, which opens onto the balcony and overlooks the tree-lined street. After crossing the bedroom and the closet, the path ends, arriving once again at the kitchen. An elevated platform under the kitchen and bathroom conceals the installations and enriches the relationship between the spaces. In the entryway, the smooth, painted cement floor continues until a wood dais in the more intimate area replaces it. The steel and glass structure of the walkway creates an aspect of lightness, while the walls that make up the interior volumes give a sensation of solidity. The mixture of textures and surfaces make this residence a rich space with a continual path.

A skylight in the kitchen, located in the center of the apartment, permits this space to enjoy natural light.

1. Kitchen
2. Bathroom
3. Dining room
4. Terrace
5. Bedroom
6. Children's bedroom
7. Hall

Previous floor distribution

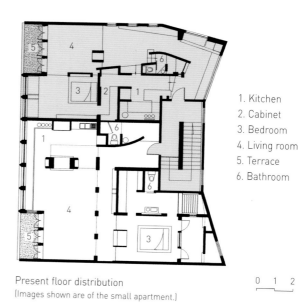

1. Kitchen
2. Cabinet
3. Bedroom
4. Living room
5. Terrace
6. Bathroom

Present floor distribution
(Images shown are of the small apartment.)

0 1 2

The great formal expressiveness of each corner of this interior is accentuated by the different textures that are achieved through the careful mix of different materials. Concrete, green marble, brick, wood, steel, and glass combine harmoniously to give each space its own personality.
The disk storage cabinets and the bookshelves form part of the interior architecture. This careful design emphasizes the play of surfaces and textures.

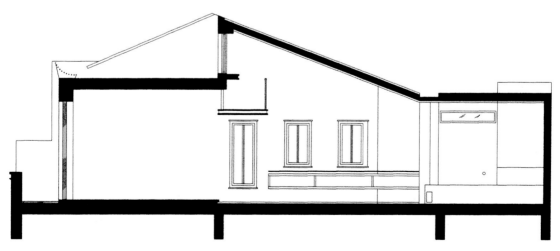

Transversal section

FORBES LOFT
LOFT

FORBES LOFT

Architect: Charles Stone
Collaborators: Foundations (constructor);
A&W Woodworking (wood)

Photographer: © Michael Moran

Location: New York, United States   Surface: 3,495 sq. ft.

This versatile distribution creates a spatial richness and a functional flexibility that allows the character of the rooms to be changed according to the varying requirements of the owners.

The central element in the renovation of this Lower Manhattan dwelling is a large structure that, besides serving as a library, dressing room, closet, and shelves, also separates the public area from the private quarters. Around the perimeter of the floor plan, there are storage modules that hide the apartment's installations (like the heating), at times interrupted to make room for benches in the dining room and living room, and to act as display pieces for art objects.

These low closets also act as a connection between the farthest areas of the loft and are the parting point for sliding doors, which enclose spaces that are normally communal, like the office, and convert them into guest bedrooms. In almost every wall of the house, there are folding or knock-down elements that create a variety of alcoves and new environments. The different areas of the dwelling are also defined by the flooring. The floor of the public area is covered with planks of recycled chestnut of varied widths; those of the kitchen and the pantry, in a freestanding module in the center of the project, are covered with white terrazzo, and the bedroom floors are sand-colored, industrially tinted felt.

Section

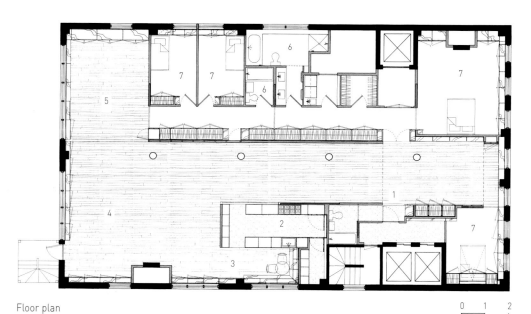

Floor plan

1. Entrance
2. Kitchen
3. Dining room
4. Living room
5. Studio
6. Bathroom
7. Bedroom

0   1   2

WAGNER LOFT

Architect: Michael Carapetian/C and C Architettura Ingegneria
Photographer: © Andrea Martiradonna

Location: Venice, Italy   Surface: 3,225 sq. ft.

A glass and stainless steel staircase guides the circulation throughout the space and terminates in the sleeping gallery which holds a suspended, circular bath tub and a glass toilet box.

Architect Michael Carapetian joined Italian architect Fluvio Caputo in 1998 to form a new limited company called C and C Architettura Ingegneria. The Wagner loft is one of their many projects completed in Italy, among other living spaces, hotels and restorations.

The residence was inserted into an industrial shell that was originally constructed in 1910 and known as the Dreher Brewery. The aim of the architect was to keep the structure intact by introducing new surfaces to sustain the rooms without removing any of the existing brick walls and wood trusses. The terraces and the lowest level of the loft are raised by a suspended steel floor and a suspended steel frame wall, dividing the space from the rest of the enveloping structure. A wood construction, in the shape of an ellipse, is cantilevered from two wood structural plates, taking up one-third of the space. This ellipse, which is reminiscent of conventional boat constructions, is comprised of prefabricated plywood box-beams. The concept and original design were developed in close collaboration with the Venetian architect Raul Pantaleo, whose contribution was fundamental in the design process, supervision of the works and selection of many artisans involved in the realization of the house. The architect's complex spatial and functional order and hierarchy of exterior, interior and interstitial spaces is reminiscent of the public and private space relationship in Venice, nonetheless the wish to keep separate the new restoration from the historical fabric of the industrial shell, was the driving concept behind Michael Carapetian's design.

A steel staircase that leads to the mezzanine consist of unique steps made of glass and steel sheets.

A freestanding shower separates the bed from the bathroom area on the top floor.

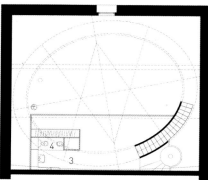

Third floor

1. Kitchen
2. Dining area
3. Bedroom
4. Bathroom
5. Living room

Second floor

First floor

0 2 4

The wooden deck terrace consists of paths and small ponds of water, an ideal place to relax and enjoy the views of distant Venice.

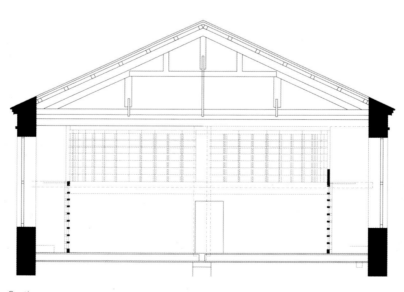

Section

OPTICAL ILLUSION

OPTICAL ILLUSION

Architect: Gil Percal

Photographer: © Gilles Gustine/Omnia

Location: Paris, France   Surface: 1,075 sq. ft.

The project's focal point was the union of the two levels via a monumental staircase that occupies the entire entrance to the apartment.

In the renovation, the architect sought to take full advantage of the natural light from the windows and their views of Parisian monuments.

A studio on the 5th floor leads to the 6th floor via the staircase that contains a blue element in the center. This item is the hidden support of the upper floor, concealing a metallic column on the left side. The aluminum texture of the stairs and the geometric play between this element and the space of the staircase creates an illusion of reversibility that alludes to drawings by M. C. Escher.

The 6th floor is the setting of a large and unified space that includes the bedroom, the kitchen, and the bathroom. The area containing the living room and the dining room is structured around the wooden ceiling frame that is asymmetrically laid out and preserves its original state. The kitchen is mounted on a dais and separated from the main space with a "wall" only 23 sq. feet. This piece of furniture, on the side of the living room, is used as a large bookcase to store, among other things, audiovisual material. The bathroom and the bedroom are located on the other side of the apartment, along with a large closet paneled in chipboard wood with stainless steel fittings.

The wood floor, the white walls, and the lighting contribute to the apartment's warmth.

This upper level apartment also benefits from the natural light of the peripheral windows and multiple skylights.

The staircase does more than resolve the structural and functional elements of the project. It also creates an attractive and fun volumetric play that entices the visitor. The cubic forms and the relations between them are more pronounced due to the innovative use of color, light, and materials. The texture of the metallic veneer contributes to the desired optical effect and creates an anti-slip surface. The same material is used to line the closet doors in the auxiliary room.

1. Kitchen
2. Bathroom
3. Dining room
4. Living room
5. Bedroom

Floor plan

0 1 2

The space is enriched by antique decorative pieces and the wooden structure of the ceiling, which was incorporated in the interior.

ORANGE AND WHITE

ORANGE AND WHITE

Architect: Pablo Chiaporri

Photographer: © Virginia del Guidice

Location: Buenos Aires, Argentina   Surface: 1,097 sq. ft.

Views between the various spaces are filtered by dividing elements, such as the large sliding wood door that constitutes one of the main decorative features of the home and disappears into the wall to permit views of the bedroom.

The interaction between the proportions of the horizontal spaces and the vertical voids, as well as the amount of natural light that fills the space, are the main resources that were used to generate the individual areas of the loft.

Dark woods, natural stone, steel, and translucent fabrics in different textures are the most prominent materials.

Neutral colors with different intensities generate a tranquil environment in which special pieces stand out.

Among a number of artworks found inside the home, the most notable pieces include the tulip chairs by Eero Saarinen, the stools by Harry Bertoia, and the original shelf piece from the 1960s by Stilka.

Comprised of comfortable furniture and bright tones of white and orange, the living area leads to the upper level, which contains the bedroom suite.

The kitchen is concealed within a module alongside the entrance hallway and incorporates a breakfast area with stools.

In the bedroom, a window behind the bed looks onto the lower level, and an en-suite bathroom reveals an open wash area and a more private shower and toilet.

The sliding door, in the same color as the rest of the accesories of the bedroom, is an important decorative element and space divider.

DESIGNER'S LOFT

Architect: Patrizia Sbalchiero

Photographer: © Andrea Martiradonna

Location: Milan, Italy   Surface: 2,140 sq. ft.

Two graphic designers decided to renovate this loft space so that they could use it as a living and work space. The studio Bauq was in charge of the restoration of the roof structure, which characterizes the style of the space.

Situated in the old naval area of Milan, this former carpenter's shop was transformed into a loft for a young couple of graphic designers and their child. The space is characterized by high ceilings that consist on one side of wooden beams and of metal sheets on the other. While these elements were conserved, new features were introduced to induce more light into the space and to better distribute the living and working space which is so important to these graphic artists who most often work from home. Given the generous height of the loft, the architect chose to divide the vertical space into two with a mezzanine level. The mezzanine is accessed by a steel and wood staircase that also divides the day and night area. The stairs wrap around a central brick pillar—a structural element characteristic to many industrial lofts—and lead to the studio whose ceiling is slightly taller than that of the remaining space. Amongst the worktables, instruments and computers, a few antique pieces stand out, such as the typographer's chest of drawers along the back wall. The pitched glass ceiling was layered with bamboo screens and draped with white fabric to diffuse direct sunlight, which in turn, is filtered through two glass panels on the floor into the dining room area directly below. Canadian pine covers most of the floor, except for traces of marble in the entrance, kitchen and bathroom. Downstairs the living area looks onto the bright orange kitchen and dining area, whose liveliness rejuvenates the antique table and chairs. The bedroom looks onto a garden terrace and incorporates an en-suite marble bathroom. The mosaic shower lies behind an acid-etched glass sheet hung from the ceiling by steel supports. The child's bedroom, which communicates directly with the parent's bedroom, comprises a world of wizards, glowing stars and moons.

The metal stain structure incorporates a table-like surface for entertainment equipment and other objects. This helps to accentuate the unity of the two levels.

Old and new: older wooden furniture is combined wih a contemporary stainless steel kitchen. The musical equipment is stowed away in the two tall orange closets that delineate the living room from the kitchen.

The studio offers a perspective of the living area while still maintaining privacy for the graphic designers.

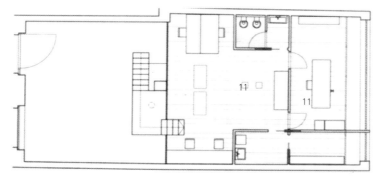

1. Entrance
2. Living room
3. Stairs
4. Dining room
5. Kitchen
6. Bathroom
7. Closet
8. Bedroom
9. Main bedroom
10. Terrace
11. Studio

Mezzanine

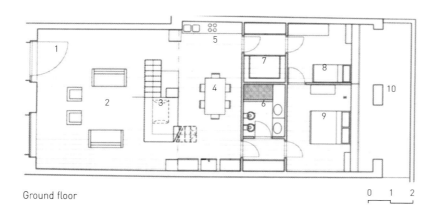

Ground floor

0   1   2

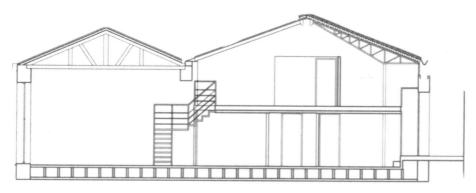

Longitudinal section

SPACE FOR TWO

SPACE FOR TWO

Architect: Guillermo Arias

Photographer: © Carlos Tobón

Location: Cartagena de Indias, Colombia   Surface: 860 sq. ft.

The transformation of this apartment into a single atmosphere with diverse functions was resolved by creating different spaces that relate to one another and define the functions of the residence. The moldings, low walls, horizontal planes, and niches were carefully studied to create aesthetic and functional harmony.

☐ This small, recreational apartment designed for a couple occupies what were once two living rooms in an old residence in a 1930s building in Cartagena de Indias. Despite the apartment's splendid views of the plaza and the church, the interior was run-down and was divided by a confusing and disorganized series of exposed beams.

The first step was to reproduce the atmosphere that most likely existed in the original space, but with a contemporary feel. A series of large moldings define the general space, which is now continual and free of dividing walls. Various architectural elements make up the different areas and disguise the central column that forms part of the structure. Just after the entrance is a space that contains the kitchen, dining room, and living room. This area ends with a window overlooking the plaza. The kitchen is designed as an isolated table that contains all of the appliances and also functions as the dining room table. A low wall, with an incorporated bookshelf, connects this space to the bedroom. A sliding door made with strips of wood and interfacing also makes it possible to divide the areas. The bathroom is found at the back of the bedroom. The headboard of the bed separates the bathroom from the bedroom and also functions as a closet. A double sink defines the bathroom's social and private areas. The toilets feature the same symmetry as the sinks, and there is a central shower. Almost all of the details of the furnishings are incorporated into the interior architecture. The architect, Guillermo Arias, designed most of the furnishings himself, including the shelves, the marble countertop in the bathroom, the kitchen cabinets, and all of the lamps. Arias is well known for his attention to detail—gestures that enrich this small space and give it formal unity.

The false depth of the walls creates a dialogue with the original spacious character of the apartment. Niches used as shelves are incorporated into the architecture itself.

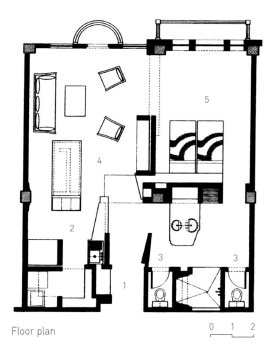

1. Entrance
2. Kitchen
3. Bathroom
4. Dining room
5. Bedroom

Floor plan

0   1   2

The lamps, designed by the architect, feature bronze, antique crystal, and alabaster, alluding to the space's original classic style.

HORIZONTAL UNIT

Architects: Stephen Quinn, Elise Ovanessoff

Photographer: © Jordi Miralles

Location: London, United Kingdom   Surface: 645 sq. ft.

The concept of chiaroscuro unifies the loft by giving the floors impact and by lightening the upper part of the atmosphere. Dark tones are used for the floors, the tables, the chairs, and everything else that makes up the lower part of the space. White, the contrasting color, is used for all of the walls, cushions, and textures of the upper part.

This apartment is located in a typical four-story Georgian house in the neighborhood of Marylebone in central London. This project entailed remodeling the first floor, which was originally a reception area. Previous renovations were of poor quality, so the architects decided to re-create the original space and adapt it to a new, more efficient use.

The apartment consisted of two different atmospheres connected with some steps. The architects first restored the large room at the front to its former size and moved the kitchen to a more convenient location. The bedroom is located in the back and leads to a walk-in closet with a sliding door painted with green-and-blue stripes. The bathroom was carefully designed to accommodate all of the necessities. The bed is made of wood and has four drawers below that complement the closet as additional storage space. As a result, the bedroom is uncluttered and gives the sensation of open space.

The furnishings in the large front room have dark tones. A desk of lacquered wood and four black chairs define the dining room, and the living room includes a sofa, in the form of an L with white cushions, and a low table. The walls are white and all of the decorative elements are limited to objects, sculptures, and statuettes placed on top of tables. Certain elements, such as the chimney and the large windows, refer to the spirit of the old house. A key feature of this project is the use of space and light, which, combined with the high ceilings, transform this small apartment into a modern and practical home. The sparse use of color mixes with the solid, dark floors to create the impression of contrast.

The finished interior of this small loft still has traces of the original Georgian house built 200 years ago. Nevertheless, the architects have managed to create a completely modern apartment with comfortable and practical surroundings.

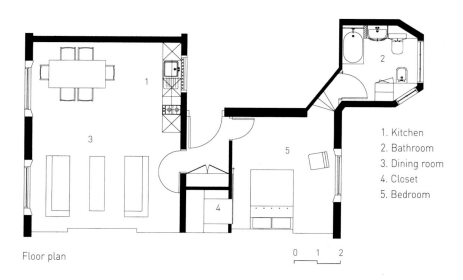

Floor plan

1. Kitchen
2. Bathroom
3. Dining room
4. Closet
5. Bedroom

0 1 2

HOUSE WITH A PATIO

HOUSE WITH A PATIO

Architect: Carlo Donati

Photographer: © Matteo Piazza

Location: Milan, Italy   Surface: 11,500 sq. ft.

The loft is articulated through three main areas: the service, day and night area. The main access leads into the spacious ten-meter-long living room that looks onto the interior patio. From here, two symmetrical, full-height doorways lead to the library and the kitchen.

This residence rises up from a narrow rectangular lot, a previously industrial site that retains only its original volume. Therefore, the transformation was realized in the interior and over its exterior skin. The volume, a single four-meter-high floor, is set within an urban fabric in which it is not possible to have perimitral apertures save for the front doors and a few windows along the street facade. The house opens entirely from within through large sliding glass doors that open up onto an elongated green garden.

The pre-existing structure was demolished and completely reconstructed copying the previous plan, thus inheriting the patio structure proper to the historical center of Milan and of contemporary architectural interventions. The generating element of the project was the patio. The possibility of creating a domestic space that was at the same time exterior is reminiscent of the classical Roman or Mediterranean home. The natural light participates by tracing the environments of the loft, its intensity changing throughout the hours of the day. The structure has the advantage of being surrounded by low-rise buildings, which separates the house from the city to such a point that it could appear to be in any other location independent from the urban context.

In order to make the most of the depth of the volume, the architect chose to directly link the different areas of the interior—swimming pool, Turkish bath, kitchen, living/dining room—so that a unique perspective could be granted from any give point inside the home.

Designer furniture by Philippe Starck, Emaf Progetti, Mies van der Rohe and Le Corbusier decorate the stylish and elegant interiors.

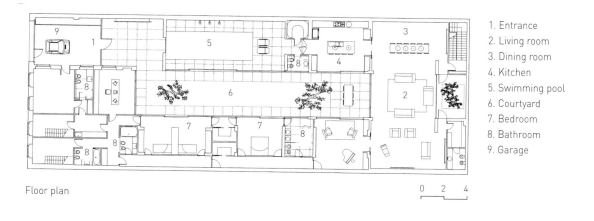

Floor plan

1. Entrance
2. Living room
3. Dining room
4. Kitchen
5. Swimming pool
6. Courtyard
7. Bedroom
8. Bathroom
9. Garage

0   2   4

The rooms are situated around the patio and are placed successively in relation to their form and function.

Playful motifs were added to the children's bathroom to evoke a young and colorful atmosphere.

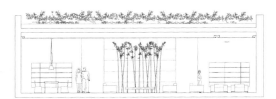

Transversal section

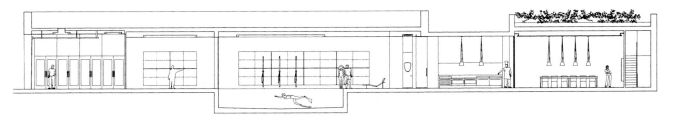

Longitudinal section

A light cream-colored stone predominates along the patio, around the pool area and inside the bathrooms.

LOFT IN AN ATTIC

LOFT IN AN ATTIC

Architect: Manuel Ocaña del Valle
Collaborators: Celia López Aguado, Laura Rojo
Photographer: © Luis Asín

Location: Madrid, Spain Surface: 376 sq. ft.

Starting with the wooden box on the terrace, everything was painted white in an attempt to instill the space with a sense of calm and to amplify the feeling of spaciousness. The furnishings, also in white, emphasize this concept and merge with the interior architecture.

What is now a comfortable, modern residence was once a small, 323 square-foot space, unsuitable for living. Located in a 150 year-old building in the up-and-coming Madrid neighborhood of Chueca, the loft provides many uses resolved in unitary and flexible spaces. The furnishings were designed as part of the architecture itself, in order to make the most of every available space. To expand the residence's useable surface area, the architect took advantage of the 15 foot-high ceilings. Under the inclined roofs, in the tallest part of the space, he divided the area into two floors, which increased the surface area by 91 square feet. The number of rooms in the loft is extensive, especially given the limited space available. The lower floor includes a dressing room, living room, dining room, kitchen, bathroom, and terrace, while the loft contains a bedroom, bathroom, dressing room, and laundry room. In order to optimize the space, it was necessary to conduct a rigorous study in order to take advantage of every square foot. The result is a playful exploration of the home that avoids traditional, rigid models. This strategy emphasizes functional flexibility. When the residents want to eat, the entire loft is a dining room; when they want to sit down, the entire space transforms into a living room; and when they want to sleep, the entire apartment is a bedroom. Technical rigor and constructional exactitude were the tools used to resolve certain aspects of the project. The apartment is located in a dirty, noisy, and disorganized urban quarter, so the project aimed to get rid of the "landscape noise" in order to create a peaceful home. To this end, the architect proposed a "noise dampener" in the form of a transitional space where the city-to-residence shift takes place.

The wooden terrace extends into the interior, producing a platform that can be used as a sofa or chair. This clever detail integrates the balcony and opens the interior space by extending it to the wooden banister.

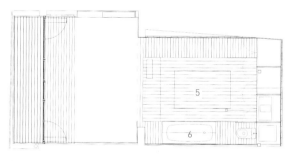

Attic floor

1. Entrance
2. Kitchen
3. Dining room
4. Terrace
5. Bedroom
6. Bathroom

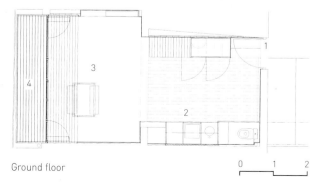

Ground floor

0   1   2

The staircase—painted white with steps that are highlighted by the color of the wood—appears superimposed on the ground floor. The space underneath the stairs is used as an auxiliary closet.

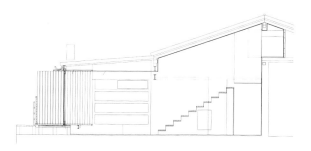 

Longitudinal sections

In the attic, the loft is separated from the bedroom by a matted, white glass screen that does not reach the ceiling or floor. This gives the space the same flexibility and amplitude as the rest of the apartment.

INSPIRED BY ICE

Architect: Marie Veronique de Hoop Scheffer
Photographer: © Virginia del Guidice

Location: Buenos Aires, Argentina   Surface: 1,505 sq. ft.

A unique interpretation of inspired techniques expresses a melange of classical, rustic, and theatrical styles.

Occupying a former Chrysler factory, this loft was designed by Marie Veronique de Hoop Scheffer, an interior designer from Belgium. Captivated by the city of Buenos Aires and inspired by the astounding glacial landscapes of Patagonia, she discovered the Palacio Alcorta, which contains some of the most beautiful lofts in the city behind its neoclassical facade.

A grand entrance announces the way into the loft. The glacier-like platform penetrates the living area and simultaneously functions as a dining table. Its similarity to a stage creates a theatrical effect, especially at night when illuminated artificially.

The entrance platform was fashioned out of slightly polished black marble from South Africa, and the floors are a light gray wood.

The colors, mainly white, blue, and gray, were chosen by the designer for their resemblance to the glaciers of Patagonia.

A staircase, designed by Marie Veronique, leads to the upper level, where a small lounge and two bedrooms are situated. Linked by a glass walkway, the two bedrooms enjoy a great deal of privacy.

A bathroom is incorporated into the main bedroom: the sinks were placed behind a counter, while the shower lies behind an opaque glass partition. The elliptical shape of the ceiling structure was preserved and emphasized by outlining the curves in blue.

White pillars punctured by glass bricks and a large gray granite platform lead down a few steps to an integrated living/dining room and kitchen.

1310 East Union

1310 East
UNION

Architects: Miller-Hull Partnership

Photographers: © Ben Benschneider, James F. Housel, Craig Richmond

Location: Seattle, United States   Surface: 700-1,600 sq. ft.

The building is a structural type of architecture that conveys a sense of economy, efficiency, discipline, and order, all of which are essential characteristics of urban loft living.

☐ Located on Capitol Hill in Seattle, Washington, this loft-style condominium project occupies a small 40 by 80 plot that was maximized by the architects' design plan. Each residential floor contains two loft units varying in size from 700 to 1,600 square feet.

The top two floors contain duplexes, one of which is shown here, with west-facing balconies, mezzanines, and shared access to a private rooftop garden.

Interior materials include concrete floors, exposed steel structural elements, steel railings, steel-plate baseboards, and modular metal kitchen casework supporting the butcher-block counters. Patches of color liven up the space.

The mezzanine on the upper level houses the bedroom and, like the lower level, has access to the private rooftop terrace.

In the interior of the lofts the large rooms are divided, based on their different uses, by the distribution of the furniture. This allows each apartment to be personalized.

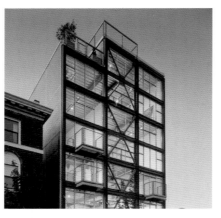

The platforms used to separate the different levels are also bare, unadorned ceilings.

Interior materials include concrete floors, exposed steel structural elements, steel railings, steel-plate baseboards, and modular metal kitchen casework supporting the butcher-block counters.

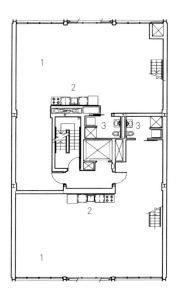

1. Dining room
2. Kitchen
3. Bathroom

Fifth floor

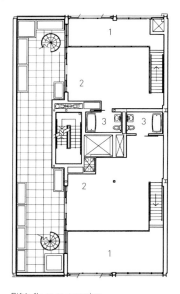

1. Void
2. Bedroom
3. Bathroom

Fifth floor mezzanine

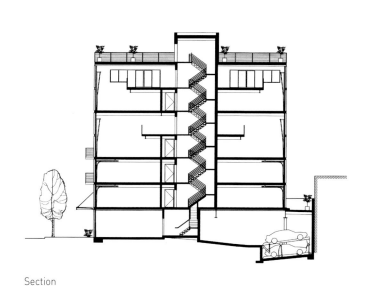

Section

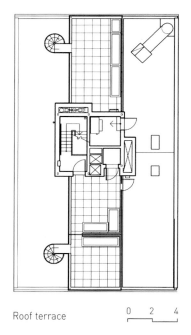

Roof terrace

0 2 4

The duplex contains integrated living/dining/kitchen areas on the lower level, which look out through a steel-framed glass facade with uninterrupted views of the city.

HOUSE INSIDE A HOUSE

HOUSE INSIDE A HOUSE

Architect: Giovanni Longo

Photographer: © Andrea Martiradonna

Location: Milan, Italy   Surface: 1,505 sq. ft.

The dwelling is at once casual and elegant. A subtle mixture of styles grants a genuinely contemporary living space.

In what was once the site of the Schlumberger factory, this attic space was rehabilitated into a living space for a young professional. The rectangular space measures 1,500 square feet and 233 feet in height. The entrance is located at one extreme and though there is but one facade, the loft receives abundant light from a pitched glass ceiling. The architectural elements were chosen for their contrasting volumes in relation to their function, and establish the different areas within a fluid, open-plan space.

The living room occupies the central area. A chimney that pierces the ceiling delineates the kitchen and dining area, which rest underneath a lowered ceiling that stops short of either side to receive the sky light. The vertical void above the kitchen is intersected by a glass panel that serves as a walkway on the upper level of the attic. A steel staircase, contrastingly lightweight in comparison to the chimney, leads to the bedroom, which is sheltered inside an independent structure for ultimate privacy and an escape from daily routine. As if it were a house inside a house, as the architects refer to it, the glass catwalk that leads to the bedroom isolates it further from the surrounding area.

Vintage and antique furniture mingle effortlessly with both ordinary and designer pieces, adding a great deal of character and personality to the home. The artworks are carefully placed in relation to the surrounding features and architectural gestures. The project consolidates an ongoing dialogue between contrasting volumes, complex forms, varying perspectives and the concept of privacy. Above all, it affords large doses of distinguished style in a remarkably subtle fashion.

The kitchen is both practical and attractive. Its U-shape allows for appliances to be kept out of sight from the living and dining area.

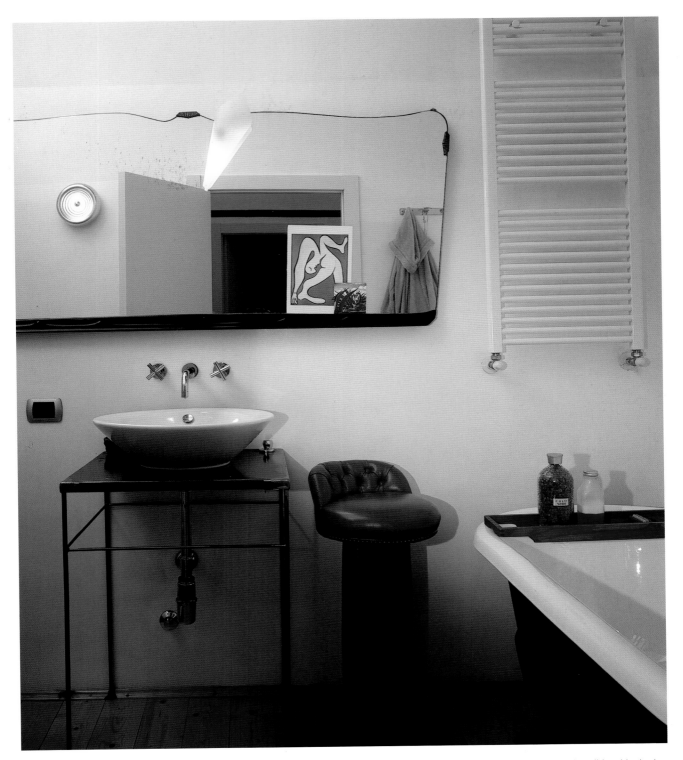

Vintage objects and art works play an important role in generating the atmosphere of this multi-faceted loft. A vintage stool and traditional bathtub sit side by side a contemporary basin design.

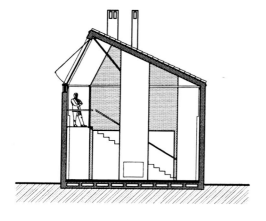

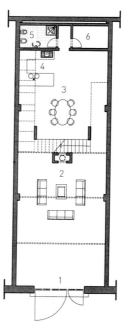

1. Entrance
2. Living area
3. Dining room
4. Kitchen
5. Bathroom
6. Guest room
7. Bedroom
8. Studio

Mezzanine

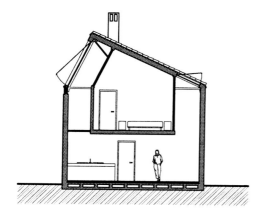

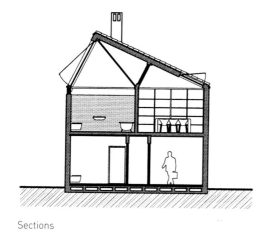

Sections

Ground floor

0   2   4

CHOIR LOFT

Architects: Delson or Sherman Architects

Photographer: © Catherine Tighe

Location: Brooklyn, United States   Surface: 1,400 sq. ft.

Harboring a volume of light and space, this loft preserves the high ceilings and wooden structure that was previously the site of a milk-distribution warehouse in the early 1900s.

The warehouse was converted into a church decades later, in the 1930s. Architects bought the neglected property and transformed it into a home for a family of four. The space was gutted out, although even the shell was in need of repair. Major structural work included rebuilding an exterior wall and bolstering existing trusses with new heavy-timber struts and steel plates.

In order to emphasize the vastness of the two-story volume, a series of deep skylights that spill light into the space was installed into the ceiling. The room was furnished with a giant 20-foot table and long bookcases.

The mezzanine, which previously was the church's choir loft, contains an intimate living area and shelters another sitting area underneath, offering cozy alternatives to the big room.

A stainless steel kitchen is a welcome contrast to the wood framework of the loft. The renovations were inspired by minimalist 1970s architecture, the building itself conveying a rough-hewn feel that is distinctly modern.

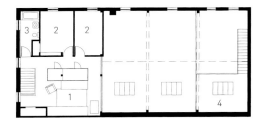

Mezzanine

1. Sitting room
2. Bedroom
3. Bathroom
4. Guest room
5. Dining room
6. Office
7. Kitchen
8. Dining area
9. Guest living room
10. Guest kitchen room
11. Studio
12. Storage
13. Laundry
14. Boiler room

Main floor

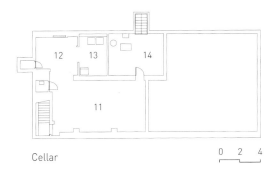

Cellar

0   2   4

Apartment on Flinders Lane

APARTMENT ON
FLINDERS LANE

Architects: Staughton Architects

Photographer: © Shannon McGrath

Location: Melbourne, Australia   Surface: 850 sq. ft.

The external appearance of the edifice has been left intact, but the interior underwent complete reform so as to reflect the frenetic activity in this area of the city.

This space is located in an old office building in the heart of Melbourne that was converted to an apartment complex. Since the building is elongated and on a corner, the apartments have windows facing the exterior, and vertical traffic is confined to the two ends. Although the exterior still looks the same as it did when the building was new—even the original windows were retained—the interior is surprising because of its contemporary design and warm atmosphere, reflecting the lifestyle in this district, which is undergoing an urban renewal process.

The project is defined by two principal elements. The first is a multifunctional, freestanding wood-framed unit that encloses the sleeping area, provides storage space, serves as an auxiliary dining room, includes bookshelves, and is a sculptural element in and of itself. This unit is self-supporting, touching neither the ceiling nor the lateral walls, and looks almost like a piece of furniture. The second element is the set of patterns sandblasted into the original cement floor. These patterns, with their polished texture, are reminiscent of the diagrams used by the architects in their design plans and contrast with the previous floor covering.

The layout is very simple. The wood-and-polycarbonate unit dynamically divides the space. On the one hand, it separates the space into two clearly defined areas: bedroom and living room.

On the other hand, it delimits the kitchen and guides traffic to the narrow entrance of the bedroom and the bathroom.

The patterns on the floor simply suggest ways to approach the layout and, to accommodate the furnishings, the area was left completely open.

In the kitchen, the wood in the furniture is combined with the cold steel of the counter cover and of the table.

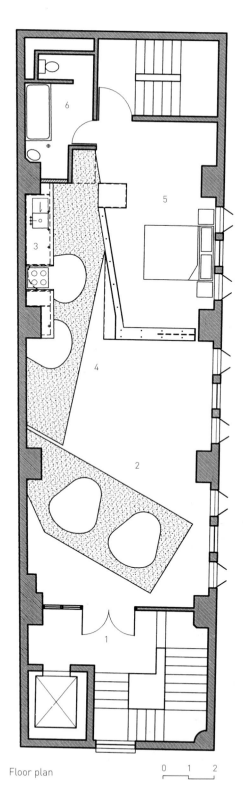

1. Entrance
2. Living room
3. Kitchen
4. Dining room
5. Bedroom
6. Bathroom

Floor plan

0 1 2

The industrial character of the space was maintained by retaining elements such as the original ventilation ducts, wrought iron, piping, and the original flooring.

ARCHITECT'S LOFT

Architect: Claudio Nardi

Photographer: © Davide Virdis

Location: Florence, Italy   Surface: 1,600 sq. ft.

The architect firmly believes that intervening in a structure like this one requires absolute reverence for the existing structural language, so that the introduction of elements does not result in an entirely inappropriate transformation characterized by an excessively thought-out design.

A plaque with the words "Construzioni Pontello 1932", just inside the home, calls to mind this building's birthday. Its reinforced concrete trusses are just one example of this period's innovative technology. The construction, much like a medieval mansion, is set amidst a non-metropolitan landscape, in the middle of a green pasture surrounded by gardens and farms. Nonetheless, it is located in the center of the city, just outside the ancient walls. The construction was and still remains one of the rare examples of industrial architecture found in the city.

The house is accessible through two paths: the first leads to the door of an art workshop, and the other to the main residence. A wooden staircase, a green path and an ancient well lead to a garden that encloses the north side of the building. The lower level, which is shared by a studio and bedroom, was designed to grant independence to each function, and places special emphasis on the strongest elements of the construction: the height, the skylight, the trusses and the light. The skylight, thanks to the horizontal division of the volume, as well as the exposed wooden beams, contribute in maintaining the atmospheric quality of a workshop. The bedrooms are situated on the two levels that stretch out over the length of the ground floor, which is designated to be the more intimate and secluded living room area.

The materials used, mainly steel, cement, plaster and glass, are raw both in terms of aspect and function. The diaphanous quality of the interior is what renders it most pure and harmonious.

A tall bookcase delineates the office area and achieves a suitable degree of privacy. Simplicity of form and material is the basis of the concept adhered to by the architect, so as not to interfere with the original character of the space.

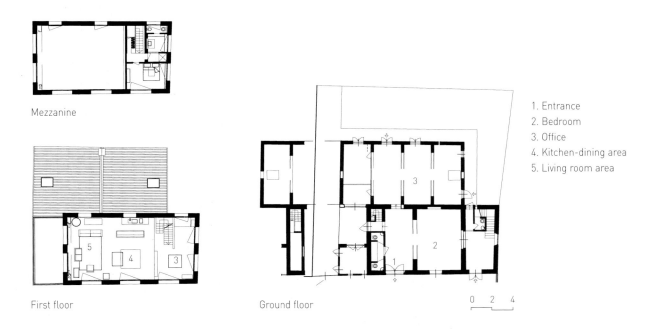

Mezzanine

First floor

Ground floor

1. Entrance
2. Bedroom
3. Office
4. Kitchen-dining area
5. Living room area

0 2 4

Large windows fill the loft with light and communicate it with the exterior patios.

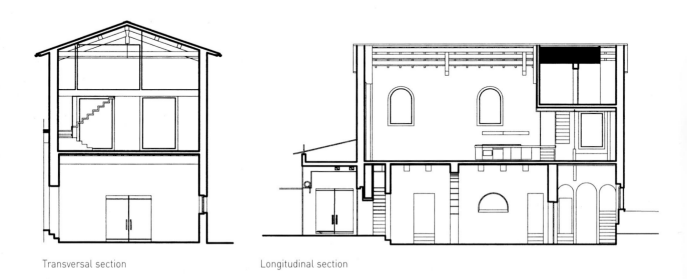

Transversal section

Longitudinal section

PHOTOGRAPHER'S APARTMENT

Architects: Tanner Leddy Maytum Stacy Architects

Photographers: © Stan Musilek, Sharon Reisdorph

Location: San Francisco, United States   Surface: 750 sq. ft.

The owner had previously converted this former paint factory into his own photography studio.

This photographer's apartment is an expansion of an existing industrial structure located on San Francisco's Potrero Hill.

The owner wanted to have the option of living there—in order to enjoy the advantages of its structure and location—but in a space separate from the work area. The original building consisted of a basic rectangular unit with structural walls of concrete block and a roof built on a framework of wooden beams. The new home, superimposed on the original structure, enjoys splendid views of the city and the bay.

The apartment is laid out as part of a series of spaces, one after the other. The studio is located on the ground floor, followed by a mezzanine and the upper floor, where the living space is located, with the roof serving as an outdoor terrace. Thus, the spaces become brighter and more open as one ascends from the closed, dark photography studio.

The kitchen and the bathroom are on a level slightly below the main space, but they are visually connected to the higher level.

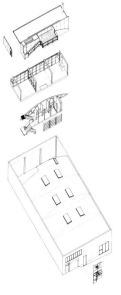

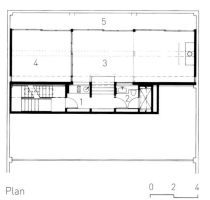

1. Entrance/kitchen
2. Bathroom
3. Living room/dining room
4. Bedroom
5. Terrace

Axonometric view   Plan   0   2   4

The narrow exterior balcony and large windows make for fabulous panoramic views of the city and San Francisco Bay.

ZARTOSHTY LOFT

Architect: Stephen Chung

Photographer: © Eric Roth

Location: Boston, United States   Surface: 2,400 sq. ft.

This loft was tailored for a bachelor who desired a space in which to relax, entertain, and host larger gatherings.

☐ Located on the top floor of a new artist loft building in downtown Boston, this project involved the conversion of a 2,400-square-foot raw shell into a primary residence.

At the owner's request, the architect designed a two-story living/dining area, an open kitchen, a wet bar, and a media room. A staircase, partly concealed behind a tall cupboard unit, leads to the upper mezzanine, which is designated to the master bedroom, bathroom, and study. A limited palette of materials was used to blur the distinction between different elements and functional areas. The cabinetry, doors, trim, and most of the flooring is dark walnut wood with a matte finish, contrasted by some walls, counters, and doors that are sandblasted glass. The remaining space is rendered in veneer plaster with a semigloss surface.

The result of this space distribution and careful selection of materials is an elegant home with minimalist details that create a serene environment.

The colors that predominate in this dwelling are both muted and light, a contrast that makes the plainness of the furniture that much more striking.

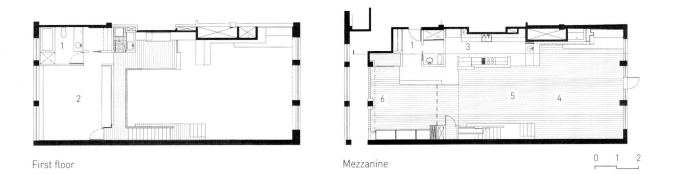

First floor

Mezzanine

0   1   2

1. Bathroom
2. Office
3. Kitchen
4. Living area
5. Dining area
6. Entertainment room

LOFT A

Architect: Carlo Donati

Photographer: © Matteo Piazza

Location: Milan, Italy   Surface: 7,150 sq. ft.

This loft-like space sprang from the unification of two apartments and a long corridor that previously led to a gallery space. Continuous spaces feature an interior pool and access to a private courtyard.

This loft is situated in a typical banister house in the center of Milan and is the result of the unification of three separate units, which consisted of two flats and a long passage that led to a wide art gallery. The challenge of the project was to link these elements to produce a coherent living space for a family. Multiple considerations, including architectural characteristics, distribution and the quality of light find a common ground to create a unique architectural project. Establishing the connection between the three entities was the first step of the design process. The long, blind corridor at the entrance was transformed into an oval foyer with two egg-shaped volumes overhead. A spiral staircase leads to the first oval on the first floor, where two bedrooms and a bathroom are located. The second oval provides access to the main bedroom, which incorporates a spacious bathroom, walk-in closet and a direct access to the private inner garden. The area designated to the living room culminates in a double-height glass atrium that contains a small swimming pool and bathroom on the first level and a mezzanine study above. The architectural choices were supported by innovative materials and avant-garde technical solutions. Corian, a type of plastic that resembles marble, was chosen for many of the furnishings. Technical solutions involved the use of carbon fibers with structural functions and the installation of the heating system underneath the floors, which also operates as a de-humidifier during the summer months. The lighting guarantees maximum flexibility–operative via remote control, personal computer or mobile phone. The project is fully equipped with the aesthetic and technical luxuries of a contemporary Italian home.

The living room space is sparsely decorated, relying on distinctive furniture, modern installations and the diaphanous quality of the loft to give character to the space.

The kitchen, dining and living areas are all visually linked and receive light from various skylights and from indirect light sources from between the walls and the ceiling.

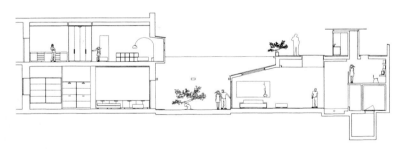

Longitudinal section

1. Entrance
2. Bathroom
3. Bedroom
4. Kitchen
5. Courtyard
6. Living area
7. Dining area
8. Swimming pool
9. Piano's room
10. Sitting room
11. Lounge room
12. Office

First floor

Second floor

0 2 4

The small pool is contained within a double-height glass wall that also incorporates a bathroom and sauna.

Soft tones play the main role in the furniture; only the red in the chairs, the curtains, and the flooring in the stairway area break this balance of chromatic values.

APARTMENT NEAR THE COLISEUM

Architect: Filippo Bombace

Photographer: Luigi Filetici

Location: Rome, Italy   Surface: 750 sq. ft.

This apartment's limited dimensions and its location close to the Coliseum were important factors to consider for its remodeling. The end result is a comfortable and harmonious home with a contemporary and elegant decoration.

This small apartment with a privileged view of one the most emblematic structures in Europe was renovated by the architect Filippo Bombace, keeping in mind its location and the urban elements that surround it. The architect opted for colors and materials that reflect the surrounding landscape: antique green and oak reminiscent of the nearby gardens of the Caelian Hill and stone gray and cardinal violet, which adorn the mural in the living area and harmonizes with the upholstery. The living and dining rooms are linked with the kitchen by a pantry that incorporates a breakfast bar. The corridor that leads to the private areas, including the bedroom and two bathrooms, was decorated with the same color palette. In the bedroom, the bed is situated underneath a small mezzanine that holds a studio. Fabrics hung vertically were used throughout the apartment to create subtle divisions without interrupting the spacious views.

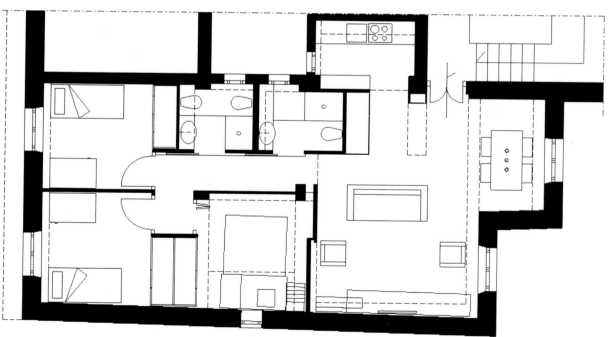

Plan

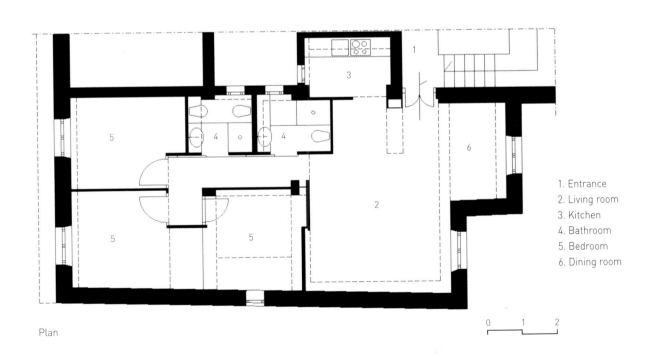

Plan

1. Entrance
2. Living room
3. Kitchen
4. Bathroom
5. Bedroom
6. Dining room

0   1   2

Section

C.E.D.V. HOUSE

Architect: Filippo Bombace
Photographer: Luigi Filetici

Location: Rome, Italy   Surface: 730 sq. ft.

This apartment was remodeled to provide a larger and more flexible home. The entrance hall clearly separates the day areas from the bedroom. The kitchen opens out onto the room and dining room creating a versatile space to receive visitors.

The owners of this residence required a flexible and spacious apartment for hosting frequent parties and informal gatherings. Originally from Naples, the owner chose the colors and materials associated with her background and opted for blue, in representation of the Bay of Naples, as the predominant color for the space. The entry leads into the main space, comprised of the living and dining areas, which is connected to an open kitchen by way of an existing opening between two suspended closets. The kitchen counter and dining table are both made of dark walnut wood. Curtains offer the possibility of isolating either of these areas. The reduced surface area was optimized through the implementation of subtle and simple divisions and the selection of few, yet sizable objects. The entrance also connects with the private areas, which can be closed off with sliding panels. The walls of the bathroom are covered with tiles that feature blue brushstrokes, and the sink rests on a walnut wood counter. Built-in faucets also save on space, and a glass door closes off the shower.

1. Entrance
2. Bedroom
3. Living room
4. Kitchen and dining room
5. Bathroom
6. Terrace

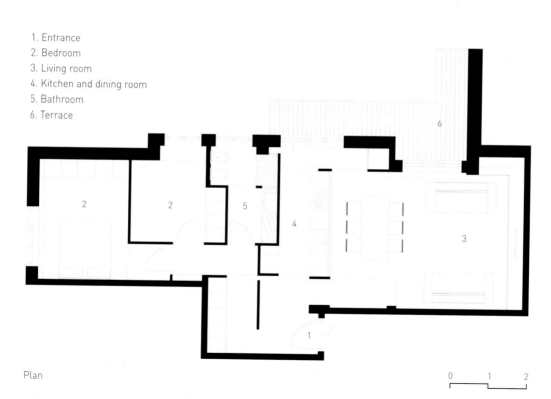

Plan

0   1   2

The bedroom has a custom-built wardrobe and paneled curtains, which help filter the light.